Land Girls at the Old Rectory

By this personal message I wish to express to you

Irene Olive Gibbs

*my appreciation of your loyal and devoted service
as a member of the Women's Land Army from*

8th June, 1942   *to*   12th January, 1946

*Your unsparing efforts at a time when the victory
of our cause depended on the utmost use of the
resources of our land have earned for you the
country's gratitude.*

Elizabeth R

Land Girls at the Old Rectory

Irene Grimwood

Old Pond Publishing

First published 2000
Reprinted 2002, 2005, 2010

ISBN 978 1 903366 00 4

A catalogue record for this book is available from the
British Library

Author's acknowledgements
Many thanks to Christine Elms for typing the manuscript, to
Tony Hare for his good advice and to all my W.L.A. friends
who shared their memories or lent photographs.

Published by
Old Pond Publishing Ltd
Dencora Business Centre
36 White House Road, Ipswich IP1 5LT
United Kingdom
www.oldpond.com

Cover design by Liz Whatling
Printed in Great Britain by the MPG Group,
Bodmin and King's Lynn
Typeset by Galleon Typesetting, Ipswich

Contents

To Edna Girling, my friend Lily Baguley and the rest of the gang who were at the Old Rectory, Halesworth with the Women's Land Army.

Foreword

WHEN the bell woke me on that rather cold, wet morning in January 1946, it was with mixed feelings that I began to dress for breakfast. I was very surprised to see that my friend Lily was not only awake, but also getting dressed, and *not* saying a word. Usually it was her lively chatter first thing in the morning that kept the rest of us awake once the bell had gone.

On this particular morning, however, both Lily and I were feeling happy one moment and sad the next. It was the last day of our service in the Women's Land Army.

As we joined the rest of the gang on the bus for work we were both in a thoughtful and nostalgic mood.

We thought of the beet we had pulled and topped, the potatoes we had picked, the miles we had cycled or motored to work.

Of aching limbs and biting north-east winds, of frozen hands and feet, and of the many times we had been up to our knees in mud and slush. On the other hand, we recalled blue skies, warm sun on our backs, skylarks singing and the smell of new-mown hay.

We thought of the farmers and their rather distant

approach when 'thousands of us town gals' had first descended on their farms. Their kindness when they got to know us better. The mugs of tea and apple pies, particularly at harvest time, and the friends we had made over the years.

Joining Up

JUST before my twentieth birthday in 1942 I decided that my war work was going to be the W.L.A. I was working at Churchman's cigarette factory in Ipswich but had always had a yearning to work in the open air. To me the Land Army seemed just right, the perfect outfit to join.

I went along to the County Hall in Ipswich where the Land Army had its office. The County Hall was a rather inspiring building, looking like a fort with turrets and battlements jutting out against the skyline and its many distinctly marked windows.

As I walked through the large gateway, I was not really nervous but had that slightly queasy feeling we all get when anticipating a new departure in life. I was rather disappointed to be told, 'Just leave your name and address and you will hear in due course.'

I am glad to say it was not long before I received a letter asking me to attend an interview. On the appointed day I went along determined to make a good impression, and as I walked into the room I noticed the pictures and posters on the walls. These were of land girls leading horses, driving tractors and doing the many jobs needed on a farm; the one that caught my eye was of a baby calf standing on lush grass in bright sunshine.

I was gazing somewhat enchanted at that delightful scene when a quiet voice behind me said, 'It won't be all baby calves and sunshine, you know.' The voice belonged to our interviewer, Mrs Sunderland-Taylor, W.L.A. County Secretary for East Suffolk.

First we were given a talk on land work in general. Then we were asked, 'Can you ride a cycle?' If we had a choice, would we prefer to do field work, dairy work or forestry? When it came to my turn I answered firmly in favour of field work. We were also asked if we would be prepared to sign on for the duration of the war. To me that was no problem.

We were then told we must have a certificate signed by our own doctors to say we were fit. Once we had filled in a form, we were free to go.

After a somewhat impatient wait I received my letter: I was now land girl Irene Gibbs, number 77475, and instructed to meet eleven other girls at Ipswich railway station on June 8th, at 2.00 pm. From there we would be going to Halesworth (also in Suffolk), where we would be billeted in the Old Rectory. The letter went on to wish me luck in my new career, and asked me to collect my uniform as quickly as possible.

I liked the walking-out uniform as soon as I tried it on. Smart and comfortable to wear, it consisted of a cream shirt, brown cord breeches, high woollen socks and very heavy brown shoes, with toe-caps and horse-shoe type studs in the heels. There were also a green V-necked pullover, a tie, a badge, and a cowboy-style hat. In winter we were issued with a delightful shorty overcoat.

I could not wait to try on the uniform at home. Unfortunately, my mother did not share my enthusiasm. She was worried that land work would be too hard for me. When my dad came home from his work as an acetylene welder I put my uniform on for him to see. My mother still seemed a bit concerned but Dad looked at me and told my mother, 'If she can stick it the first week or two, she'll be all right.' I was determined not to let my dad down.

My sister Ivy told me a friend of hers had joined the W.L.A. and was going to Halesworth on the same day I was. Her name was Lily Baguley, and it was arranged that we should look out for each other at the station. I was looking forward to meeting her as Ivy said she was great fun to be with. In fact, June 8th could not come quickly enough.

The big day arrived at last and as I made my way to the station, I hoped very much that Lily and I would get along all right. However, when I got to the station ten girls were already there none of whom answered to her name. The train puffed its way along the platform, but still no sign of her. Rather disappointed I got on the train. Then, just as the guard was blowing his whistle, I saw a land girl running along the platform. Our door was quickly opened and one breathless female and her case came hurtling in. She flopped down onto the seat and with a grin said, 'Hello everyone, I'm Lily.'

At Halesworth we were met by a woman in her mid-thirties, wearing a W.L.A. uniform but with a green beret instead of a cowboy-type hat. She shook us firmly by the hand and welcomed us to the Land Army. 'Right girls, my name is Mrs Bilson and I am your forewoman. Well come along, you can put your cases in my van, then you can walk to the Old Rectory. It isn't far, you can't miss it. Turn right at the end of this street, then right again at Rectory Lane. Go up there and you'll see the Rectory on your left.'

As she got into her van she added, 'By the way, girls, as I said my name is Mrs Bilson, but everyone calls me Billy, so you may as well get used to it,' and with a wave she had gone. We were not all sure what to make of 'Billy'; she was very direct and to the point, one who would stand no nonsense! I think we were all beginning to have doubts as to whether we would like being land girls and it was twelve rather quiet individuals who set off for the Old Rectory.

The old Suffolk house with its enormous tiled roof and dormer windows was down a drive lined with trees and bushes. Its uneven walls were painted pale cream and in the front was a welcoming porch with a large brown door.

As soon as the building came into view, my misgivings were dispelled. I liked what I saw and had the lovely warm feeling that I was going to be very happy living here. Three girls from the Beccles area were already in residence so that made fifteen of us, and when the Rectory was full it would house thirty.

Billy instructed us to take our cases upstairs and to pick which bedroom we liked. Lily and I chose one with six beds, our other room-mates being Molly, Joan, Audrey and Nella, all from Ipswich.

Friendly and outgoing, Molly had been manageress of a wool shop. Her father was a merchant navy captain who was to be awarded the Croix de Guerre after the war. Joan, whose parents kept the County Hotel was quiet and dignified. Audrey was engaged to be married and Nella, in her mid-thirties, was the eldest of us. She had been housekeeper for her aunt and uncle and had a good sense of humour that was later to be pushed to its limits when Lily put a live frog down her neck. The youngest of us, Lily had been a machinist making army uniforms. She had decided to volunteer for the W.L.A before she was called up for munitions work.

The bedroom was not large but it was big enough for the six small wooden beds, a locker each and a small wardrobe between two. I did not think we were going to be very comfortable sleeping on the straw palliasses that adorned our beds but I expect that was the idea: they wanted us to be glad to get up in the mornings! We unpacked and went downstairs where we were given tea. We met our warden, Mrs H., and Anne who would be our cook.

Later on, Lily and I went for a quick look round before settling down for the night. When we got back we went into the kitchen to see what was for supper. It was bread and cheese and hot, thick cocoa. 'It's the same every night,' we were told. There was a portion of butter put out; a case of first come, first served as far as that precious commodity was concerned. The late ones went without. Apart from a few times Lily and I were rarely back in time to get any butter but there was always plenty of bread and cheese.

After lights out the six of us talked quietly for a time, then said our goodnights and settled down. I had no sooner dozed off than I was jolted awake by a loud thud! Lily had fallen out of bed. The warden came hurrying in, demanding to know what all the noise was about. Lily told her she was used to a double bed at home and in turning over had fallen on the floor. 'And what is your name girl?' snapped the warden. 'It's Lily.' 'Well Lily, and the rest of you, you'd better get some sleep, you have a hard day's work ahead.' The light was put out and the door firmly closed.

As I settled down for the second time, I was sure that life with my new friend Lily was going to be eventful and a great deal of fun.

It seemed I had no sooner got to sleep when I was woken by a large handbell, rung with great force in the doorway. 'Time to get up, Girls!' bellowed a stentorian voice. It was 6.00 am; it seemed like the middle of the night! At 6.30 another bell was rung, this time to summon us down to breakfast.

After breakfast we had until 7.00 am to make our beds, stand our lockers on top of them, then go into the kitchen to collect flasks of tea or coffee and small lunch tins containing sandwiches, a bun or rock cake, an apple or whatever fruit there was available. We were then ready for work, in our working outfit of dungarees and matching jacket, woollen socks and heavy black lace-up farm boots.

The First Day's Work

BILLY told us that hoeing was our job for June, and that we would be working with the W.A.E.C. (War Agriculture Executive Committee) men, who would provide the transport. We were not impressed when the transport turned out to be an open lorry with about nine grinning W.A.E.C. men of various ages on board. One of them jumped down, lowered the tailboard and helped us up.

It was a very bumpy ride, and one of our number, Peggy Richer, was not very well. Billy made her sit quiet for a time.

We got to our destination and started work, and believe me hoeing a large field was very different from a small garden back home. Our hands soon got very sore and blistered. Seeing our plight, the farmer gave us a good tip: 'Tomorrow morning, Gals, before you start work, spit well on both hands. You'll find they won't get nowhere near as sore.' This did prove to be sound advice.

Billy came to each of us in turn, first to teach us how to stand, which was very important for our backs. Then she showed us how to get rid of the weeds without harming the plants, and also how to single them out.

That first day seemed to go on for ever. It was very hot, our boots were hard and made our ankles very painful, and muscles that were not used to such strenuous activity were rudely awakened from their inertia. Our breaks could not come quickly enough – what bliss it was to find a bit of shade and have a rest.

At the end of that first day, aching all over, how glad I was to get back to the Rectory and luxuriate in a nice hot bath before our evening meal. Well, actually I had to make do with five inches of water as that was all we were allowed. To solve this problem we later got in two at a time and when we got to know each other better we even had four girls to a bath; two sitting in the bath and two with their feet in the water. It was much quicker that way, if somewhat lacking in hygiene.

After a few weeks I got up one morning and realized I did not ache any more. What a relief, I felt like a real land girl at last. But there was still the journey on that bone-rattling lorry to contend with.

Then one day the men told us with a great deal of pride that they had now got hold of a bus and would pick us up with it the following Monday. Well, we could not wait, and the next Monday we girls were all gathered at the top of the drive, waiting for this last word in transport to arrive. We could not believe it. It was old, dirty and most of the windows were missing. Mind you, we soon realized the missing windows were to our advantage, as most of the men smoked the most revolting smelling tobacco in their pipes.

Once when we had rather a long way to go and the journey was beginning to get a bit boring, we had quite a diversion. The man sitting next to Lily knocked the contents of his pipe into her jacket pocket, which was beginning to smoulder quite alarmingly. Lily jumped to her feet shouting that she was on fire. Billy hauled her off the bus and got rid of the ash. We girls alighted (rather an appropriate word in the circumstances) and refused to get on again unless we could all sit together. Billy had a word with the men, then ordered us back on board. The men were all sitting on one side and we girls sat on the other. The men grinned all the way to work.

Not long after that incident we came home one day to find a Grey/Green London coach in the drive complete with driver, Jack Seagul, who lived in the out-buildings at the Old Rectory and had his meals in the kitchen. He stayed until the Rectory closed in 1945. Having our own transport was much more convenient.

On really hot days Billy would put an urn of water on the bus for us as our flasks were soon empty. On one such day two of our girls fainted from the heat, and when Billy went to the urn to get them a drink, she found it empty. She and Jack took the urn to fill it at the nearest source which happened to be a couple of fields away. They duly filled the urn and brought it back. We had a drink or two during the afternoon and felt refreshed.

On the way home Billy enquired after our health; did we all feel well? She was very relieved to learn we were all fine because the only water she had been able to find was in a rather murky pond containing a lot of foreign bodies. But not to worry, Jack had strained the water through his handkerchief. I think we felt ill after that statement, but there were no after effects.

After hoeing came hay-making, a job I enjoyed very much. Turning the hay with blue skies above as skylarks sang was bliss. There was nothing to equal it. Later we bundled the hay on to carts which took loads to the yard, where the stacks were built. The hay was then ready for the farmer's needs.

On one of those pleasant, happy days we decided a shandy would go down a treat with our sandwiches. We asked a young lad whom we were working with if there was a pub nearby. 'Just down the road a bit,' he told us

That was good enough for us. At midday we set off. We walked along with not a care in the world. I glanced at my watch and was surprised that we had been walking for twenty minutes without a pub in sight.

Two women talking at their gate gave us the same answer to our query. We should then have turned back. We had an hour's break for lunch, but we had now been walking for more than thirty minutes. However we kept going but now we were running. A man walking his dog told us, 'It isn't far. Just down the road a bit.'

At last the pub came into view. We dashed in and gasped out, 'Five shandies please', thankfully found some empty seats and sank in them. The barman brought over our drinks. He seemed very concerned. 'Well my dears, if I were you, I should sit quiet for a while before you drinks these.' We took his advice. After all, what was the point of rushing? We would be at least an hour late back.

We were in trouble. We enjoyed our drinks, walked back to the field and a good ticking off. We had to work very hard all afternoon to make amends. One valuable lesson we learnt that day was, 'just down the road a bit,' could mean anything from five minutes to an hour's walk.

Hitch-Hiking

MONEY never seemed to go anywhere. We were always short. When our board and lodgings were deducted along with the 6*d*. which we had to pay into the benevolent fund, we had very little left. What to do about it, that was the question?

Five of us – Barbara, Ruby, Edna, Lily and I – decided to hitch-hike next time we were going home for the weekend. That would save our rail fare. We all lived in Ipswich and that meant we could all keep together. The following Saturday we set off. We had a small weekend-case each, and in addition Lily had a meat tin for her mother. Meat tins were very hard to get in wartime. Lily had spotted this one in the hardware shop and had dashed in to get it before it was snapped up.

At first nothing came along, then a sports car stopped. 'Can I give two of you a lift?' offered the driver.

'No thanks, we are all together,' was my reply.

But before anything else was said Ruby and Edna got in the car. As it was only a two-seater it was a bit of a squeeze for them, so imagine the driver's astonishment when we three girls jumped on the back of the car – Barbara one side, I the other and Lily cling-ing on as best she could in the middle.

The car shot off at great speed and a second later Lily, accompanied by one case and one meat tin, landed with a clatter on the road. I shouted to the driver to stop but he just carried on for a bit. He then halted, told Barbara to get off and shot off again before I could put my feet on the ground. By now I was beginning to get a bit panicky and when the car stopped further on and I was told to get off, it was with great relief I did so.

I sat by the roadside and waited for the other two to catch up. We then ran in the direction the car had taken and soon came to Ruby crying by the roadside. The four of us were very concerned about Edna. Had she been kidnapped? We feared the worst and began to run. A little way along the road we were relieved to see Edna, fed up with having to wait for us but otherwise unharmed. We were very careful after that fright and made sure we all kept together.

Back at the Rectory on Sunday we got a right ticking off from Billy for getting lifts the previous day. The chap in the sports car was a friend of hers and had telephoned to let her know that we were hitching lifts and also that he had dropped us off apart, to deter us. He hoped we would get the train home in future.

For a time it did put us off but then we decided to have another try. We got lifts in all types of vehicles but the two I remember most were a black Ford car and a fish lorry.

The car took us to Saxmundham. It was a bit of a squeeze with five girls and five cases, plus the driver's case. At our destination Lily got out first and I handed her our luggage. We thanked the driver, picked up our belongings and walked up the street. Glancing back we realized a case was left on the pavement – it was the driver's! Lily picked it up and ran in the direction the car had taken. Luckily for us he went into a garage along the road. He got quite a surprise when his case was handed back to him.

When we had a lift with the fish lorry, we had to sit at the back amongst the fish. The smell was awful. My mother could not stand it, so everything was washed, breeches on the line all weekend, but still the smell remained. In fact it was a week or two before it finally cleared.

After some successful journeys we got so confident, that one Sunday evening the five of us decided to get lifts from Ipswich back to the Rectory. We started full of optimism and all went well at first, with a lift to Woodbridge and another to Saxmundham. Then, nothing. We waited and waited, but nothing came along. We were in trouble! We decided to get a taxi. Barbara looked for a door with a taxi plate and knocked. 'Could you please take us to the Old Rectory, Halesworth?'

The man peered at us. 'Are you land girls?'

'Yes we are.'

'I am not turning out for land girls at this time of night,' and the door was shut with a bang.

The only thing to do was to telephone the warden and tell her of our plight. Barbara took charge and the warden was duly informed. She was not a happy woman. 'Start walking immediately and report to me when you get here.'

The night was dark and eerie and a twelve-mile walk did not appeal to us at all. Feeling somewhat disenchanted we left Saxmundham behind. We discussed the situation and what to do for the best. It was decided that if a vehicle came along we would get on it no matter what direction it was taking. With that settled we strode on towards Halesworth.

Some time later we saw dimmed headlights coming towards us. We shouted, waved and danced up and down. It was a bus. It stopped and a very irate voice told us to get on and be quick about it. The warden had woken Jack and sent him to pick us up. He was not amused. We were told to sit quiet and that the warden was waiting up for us. We did not relish the telling-off we were about to get. When we reached the Rectory the very angry warden told us to get to bed and make sure we were up at first bell in the morning.

Next day a notice was put up that warned about

the dangers of hitch-hiking. For a time it was the train for us. Then the urge came to have one more try at getting lifts from Ipswich to Halesworth.

It was a fine Sunday night and at first things went well until, as you have guessed, Saxmundham. This time we did not hesitate but found another taxi and we were in luck. We arrived at our destination with ten minutes to spare. We went into the kitchen, had our bread and cheese and went to bed.

However, the warden spotted us in the kitchen with our cases and guessed we had not come on the train. Nothing was said to us, but head office was informed and a few days later a very large notice was put up: HITCH-HIKING IS FORBIDDEN. It was fun while it lasted, but it was the train for us girls from now on.

Harvest Time

THE last week in July was the start of harvest time when the clocks were put on two hours to give the farmers as much light as possible for the gathering-in of the crops. With a war on it was vital to grow as much as we could, and the more we grew, the more there was to be harvested.

Most farmers had the old-type cutters and binders. Combine harvesters were a rare sight in those days, though I did see one during my land army career, and what a silver monster it was!

On our first day our job was to watch while a scythe was being used to cut a pathway round the field so the binder could start. We were told to have a turn with the scythe, with an added warning to jump if we felt the tool slipping, otherwise it might cut our legs off. It only took one mistake for a girl's career and body to be shortened in one fell swoop!

With its long, heavy handle and regularly sharpened blade, the scythe gave me some scary moments. However, most men and boys on the farm could use one, so of course, not to be outdone, we land girls had to persevere. Eventually I mastered it.

Walking round the field stooking (or as some called

it, shocking) was a hot and tiring job. Shocking or stooking meant taking a sheaf of wheat under each arm and standing them up in eights.

Rabbits were in great abundance during the war. When the field was almost cut and only a diamond shape was left, the dogs were let loose and the men with their guns moved in. The dogs were in their element routing out the poor little bunnies. There was much shouting and cussing. Men ran around like boys; dogs and rabbits everywhere. Total chaos.

Although the farmer told us to give a shout if we saw any rabbits getting away, we could not do it. When we saw one of the small creatures hiding under a sheaf it looked so scared that Lily merely picked it up and gently put it over the hedge. Unfortunately, the farmer saw this act and gave us a right ticking off. 'Don't you know how to catch one of the little so and sos? You're not here to rescue the little blighters but to catch them.' Soon dozens of rabbits had been caught. The farmer was happy and it was back to work for us.

The main crops were wheat, barley and oats. When it came to pitching, wheat was the heaviest with barley and oats being much lighter. The snag with barley was the awns which got everywhere. At this time of year it was usually very hot so most of us girls rolled our sleeves and trouser legs up to keep cool. Billy told us off for having bare legs and arms but it was better to be cool than to worry about a few scratches.

It was very thirsty work and our flasks were soon empty. We were often given a drink at work, mostly a mug of tea which went down very well. Sometimes it was cider which went down even better, more so if it was the strong sort, then work seemed wonderful, and I must say a lot of work was got through.

During the 1943 and 1944 harvests Lily and I worked together on the same farm, a short cycle ride from the Old Rectory. By then there were Yanks stationed just up the road from the farm. Their radar station was in the middle of the farmer's barley field. They often came to help with the harvest and gave Lily and me chocolate, candy, cracker biscuits and our first taste of canned drinks.

During the harvest of 1943 I had a most unfortunate accident. I was loading a cart with Peggy Todd. We got the distribution slightly wrong, so when the horse moved off the load slipped, taking Peggy and me with it. We hit the ground with a thud. Peggy hurt her leg but after a rest she was able to go back to work, although she had a few bruises later on. As for me, I had twisted my foot and could not put it to the ground. No one could be spared from the farm so I had to make my own way back as best I could. It was hard cycling with one foot, but I eventually got back to the Rectory. At the doctor's surgery my foot was tightly bandaged and I was instructed to keep off it for three weeks. I stayed on at the Rectory but in fact it was six weeks before I could walk on the foot and go back to work.

Another potentially serious accident had happened when a gang of us were working with Flo who was driving a tractor and pulling a trailer with us on it. Halfway across the field the trailer became unhooked. While Flo carried on blissfully unaware, the trailer with us aboard was gathering speed and heading towards the hedge.

Blondie shouted to us to jump and we all leaped clear seconds before the trailer crashed. Flo came racing back to see if we were okay, then hooked the trailer back on to the tractor. She waited for us to climb up. 'No thanks Flo,' we said. 'We'd rather walk. It's safer that way.'

Summer had passed and it was now autumn, bringing with it new jobs: potato picking and pulling, and topping sugar beet. It was good to be back at work after my foot had mended. Two things of interest happened in October. First my young sister Elsie joined the W.L.A. At 17 years and 4 months, she was the youngest in our group. She was sent to the Old Rectory, Henstead which was rather isolated and involved a five-mile cycle ride to Beccles to catch the train to Ipswich.

The second interesting item was that the Yanks

arrived at Holton airbase, a short walk from Hales-worth. Now our peaceful little town was quiet no longer. Yanks were everywhere, chewing gum, calling all the girls Honey, shouting Hi to anyone who cared to listen. The pubs were crowded and often short of beer. On the plus side, we had invitations to their dinners and dances and we were never short of an escort.

As Christmas approached, Lily and I were working on a farm near the Rectory. The farmer kept ducks and chickens. We asked if we could each buy a bird for our mothers. 'You had better come to the barn and pick one,' he said. I soon picked mine. Lily said her Mother would like a duck. 'Well Missie, come with me.'

We went into the yard where the ducks were running about making a lot of noise. 'Point out which one you like.' As soon as Lily pointed one out, the farmer picked it up, wrung its neck and gave it to her. Seeing her ashen-faced distress he soon took the bird off her and told us to collect them the afternoon we were going home

We got a nice surprise when we went to pick up the birds, because the farmer also gave us a dozen eggs, some holly, mistletoe and a small Christmas tree each. We had not told our mothers about the gifts. What a happy Christmas it was that year!

Animals and Me

I MUST admit I was very nervous of animals, and after a year I was only a little less afraid. On one farm we were told we all had to lead the horse in turn. I felt very scared when it was my turn. I stood as far away from the animal as I could. The farmer stood watching me for a while, then called out, 'Missie. Is that horse leading you, or are you leading the horse? Get a bit nearer, it won't bite you.'

Very frightened, I did as I was told. Somehow the horse knew I was nervous and behaved perfectly. My confidence grew and I felt very chuffed by the time I got to the end of my turn. From then on I have had a great respect for horses.

Now a bull was a different matter! Barbara, Sybil, Vera, Lily and I were five very new land girls on Mr C's farm when he told us to be sure to go to the house at midday for a cup of tea. 'Take a short cut across the field, the cows won't take any notice of you Gals.'

At midday we set off. At first all went well until Barbara saw that one of the cows had left the herd and was trotting behind. She gave a shriek, 'Run, it's a bull!' We ran, and didn't stop until we got to the five-barred gate and just threw ourselves over it. We dashed to the house and hammered on the door.

'Whatever is the matter?' asked Mrs C.

'Your bull chased us,' we managed to gasp.

Mrs C. looked out of the door. 'That's not a bull, it's Daisy. She won't hurt you, she wouldn't hurt a fly. Sit down and I'll make you a nice cup of tea.' We drank our tea and went back to work feeling rather foolish, wondering what Mr C. would have to say when he found out.

However, nothing was said although we got some very thoughtful looks during the afternoon.

Next day when we arrived for work, Mr C. was waiting with his bike at the top of the drive.

'Keep on your bikes, Gals, and follow me.' Rather puzzled, we cycled after him to the next farm. We went into the yard where we saw a very large bull chained up. 'Now Gals, that field we passed was full of cows, right? Well this here is a bull. Now I want you to take a good look and in future I hope you will be able to tell the difference. Well come along, can't stand here all day, we have work to do.'

It was five rather red-faced girls who followed him back up the lane. One good thing, we now knew what a bull and a cow looked like.

Geese were a real problem on one farm where every morning a flock of them came to meet us squawking and flapping their wings. We were all

of their walking-out uniforms. Clockwise from the top left: Peggy Todd; the 20-year-old author; Wilson and Peggy Richer; Barbara Moyes.

Jack Seagul, driver of the Grey-Green bus with some of the girls at work.

Rectory girls in 1942. Mrs Billson (Billy) is on the extreme left; eighteen-year-old Edna Girling who
soon to be killed in a tragic farm accident is three girls along from her on the front row with Lily to t
left and the author to the right

Clockwise from top left:
the author and Bobby, a farm dog;
Lily Baguley with a horse and tumbril;
Joyce Berry and tractor driver
Flo Stone with helpers.

Outside the Old Rectory in July 1942. L-R back row: Molly Leeks, Lily Baguley, Audrey Cr
Kathy Burnes, Joyce Berry, Elsie Gardener, the author, Joan Wilson, Doris Simp

Jella Preston, Gladys Chapman, Vera Elsey, Joan Travers, Rosina Gedge. Middle row: Flo Stone, Front row: Joyce Long, Ruby Smith, Edna Girling, Irene Watson, Pearl Hurren, Peggy Richer.

In walking-out uniforms of fawn shirt, cord breeches, high woollen socks, heavy brown shoes, green pullover and land army tie: Rosina (Butchy) Gedge, Joan Wilson, Peggy Richer and Irene (Bungay) Watson

In dungarees and coats, pausing in front of a stack.

...d Woolton reviews the Land Army parade in August 1943 at the Cornhill, Ipswich.

...ck to work, forks at the ready..

The rear of the Old Rectory with the recreation room on the ground floor and the author's bedroom the first floor, left. How did she climb out of that window?

The author looking over the rectory wall in 1999. With her are Lily (right) and a friend. Lily's daughter took the photograph.

scared and would free-wheel down the drive with our feet on the handle-bars.

Smaller creatures could also be frightening. One day when Lily and I were working in the same field, she drag-raking while I was trimming the bank, my slasher hit a wasps' nest. I heard a loud buzzing and all at once wasps were everywhere – on my face and in my hair. I frantically picked them off and could not believe it when they all just flew away.

I stood shaking for a minute or two and then realized that although the drag-rake and horse were standing near the hedge, Lily was nowhere to be seen. When I ran into the next field she was just getting to her feet. The horse had taken fright at the wasps and had not stopped until it reached the hedge, throwing Lily over it. She had landed with a thud on the other side.

A week later a lone wasp flew down and stung me on the finger. It was very painful and made me realize how lucky I had been the previous week.

Most farms had dogs. I was very wary of them, but learned to walk by and just be friendly. As for the farm cats, all they were interested in was resting in the barn or chasing mice around.

The Old Rectory

I ENJOYED my stay at the Old Rectory very much. It was three years and three months of pleasure.

There was a driveway with trees and bushes either side and around most of the house was a large lake which had everything from tadpoles to a family of moorhens. There were flowerbeds, lawns, fruit trees and a vegetable garden. There were also a few out-buildings and a shed where we kept our bikes.

The house was old, mysterious and very intriguing. The bedrooms were of various sizes, the largest having eight beds. This room had quite a large fire-place with a wide chimney. Were little boys in days gone by sent up to sweep it, we wondered? A bedroom door at the top of the house had seven key-holes. We never found out the reason for that, or why the cellar floor and cold slab in the walk-in pantry were gravestones. It certainly gave us girls an odd feeling to see butter and cheese resting on *In loving memory of Alice* or was it *Emma*?

The recreation room was very comfortable with easy chairs, books, and a piano. A good sized dining room had a serving hatch so Anne Frost, our cook, could pass our meals through.

We enjoyed a lot of Anne's food, but not all of it. Breakfast was quite good: bacon, eggs, porridge, fried bread and toast, not all together of course. We did have eggs and bacon about three mornings a week. Our evening meals were also excellent, Anne being a very good cook.

It was the food during the day which left much to be desired. Four small sandwiches, a rock bun or cake and any fruit available. This had to last us all day, plus a flask of tea or coffee. The sandwiches were either meat, cheese or jam. The first two items were not too bad, apart from one time when the lamb was maggoty. It was awful, but the birds got a treat that day! Poor old Jack had eaten his during the morning. I bet he could not look at a meat sandwich for a very long time. Billy took one look at hers and dashed off in her van after telling us not to eat anything. She came back with some large bags of buttered rolls. We asked no questions but just tucked in.

The hostel's cat, George was a liability where the jam sandwiches were concerned. He was long-haired, white and fluffy, and his favourite place was the kitchen. By lunchtime our jam sandwiches were not only dry and curled up, but they often also had George's hairs in them. Ugh! The hairs showed up more in the jam than on meat or cheese. Supper was always the same: bread, cheese and cocoa plus any chips we brought in with us.

There were thirty of us girls at the Old Rectory, all thrust together due to the war. Our everyday life changed completely. We were now living away from our homes and families and answerable to a warden. I will say this, we all got along quite well together, although there could be little disagreements.

I remember Gladys having to put her socks out on the window-sill at night because the girls in her room thought they were a bit smelly. One weekend she left her spare socks at home. Next night it rained, resulting in wet socks the following day. Refusing to put them out again, Gladys shoved them under her bed – problem solved.

We were told by the locals that the Rectory was haunted. A monk on horse-back would gallop round the grounds at midnight. Beware, we were told, dire things would happen if we were awake at midnight and heard the horse.

We dismissed this as a joke and forgot about it, until one night a few weeks later, Lily woke up in a panic. The cause of her fear: a *horse* galloping round the grounds! We told her not to play games and to go to sleep. Then, all of us heard it. Lily was right. Fear and apprehension abounded. We were so scared we slept two in a bed. It was a tight squeeze and no one got much sleep. Morning could not come soon enough.

Billy's remark of, 'My word, you do look a bright

lot this morning,' did not help at all as we went into breakfast. We were all suffering from fright and lack of sleep owing to the ghost horse cantering around in the night. 'Well girls, you can put your mind at rest, there is no ghost, it was the sweep's horse. Somehow it got into the grounds. Mr Brown has just been to fetch it.' We got a lot of funny looks and winks in the pub that night and realized someone had played a trick on us.

Some of the most embarrassing things we had to contend with at the Rectory were the bumby lavatories put up in the orchard because there were not enough inside the house. They were wooden seats with a bucket, partitioned off by thin wooden panels.

One day a week the bumby cart came to empty the pails. As we never knew at what time in the evening the men would come, the lavatories were very often being used when they arrived. The men would then knock loudly on the doors, 'Hurry up Gals, the cart is here.' The doors would open and a few very red-faced girls would appear and make a quick dash for the house.

Relaxation

IT WAS important to relax after a hard day's work, and we had various ways of doing this. Over the years we filled the pubs and drank many pints of shandy.

We could visit the Old Picture House with its corrugated iron roof and a few seats for courting couples. It was wise to be prepared in wet weather as the roof leaked. When it rained heavily the noise of the raindrops on the iron roof was so great that you could not hear what was being said on the screen. To liven things up, a mouse was often to be seen running around. We girls mainly kept our feet off the floor.

Others preferred a stroll with a boyfriend or a visit to the Old Canteen (later replaced by an Anglo-American canteen) where we enjoyed beans on toast, a cup of tea and a good gossip. Some just liked reading or staying in washing their hair.

Hair washing became a more serious matter on Molly's return after a weekend at home. Seeing her scratching her head a lot Molly's mother found that her daughter had nits. No amount of pleading would persuade her to allow Molly to return to the hostel on Sunday. Instead, come Monday morning, she marched Molly into the W.L.A. office, demanding irately that 'something be done about these damned nits my daughter has picked up.'

As it happened, Molly was not alone. Barbara walked in with her mother and the same complaint. When the mothers had given the name of the hostel and had been calmed down they were assured that something would be done forthwith.

Both girls were kept at home while things at the hostel were sorted out. As for the rest of us, we had no idea what was going on. All we knew was that two girls had not returned on Sunday.

On Tuesday the warden gave an order for us to be in the recreation room at 7.00 pm prompt. We were making guesses as to the reason for her request when in marched the warden carrying a kidney-shaped basin containing some vile-smelling lotion, a large steel comb and a very determined look on her face.

'It has come to my notice that we have nits. Well, I shall soon get rid of them. Nits indeed! Come along now, line up. This won't take long.'

Having shoulder-length hair, I was not looking forward to it. I washed my hair twice after, but the smell lingered on and on.

To our relief the epidemic was soon cleared up, although the warden would still have a nit inspection whenever she thought about it. Thankfully, as the months went by the situation was forgotten.

One evening Lil and I wanted to have a quiet drink

on our own and avoid our dates who were waiting for us at the gate. We decided to nip across the garden, get over the wall and drop down away from the gate into the lane.

It did not quite work out as planned. Although the ground was higher on the Rectory garden side, on the lane side we were faced with a six-foot drop. However, we thought, 'here goes.'

Lily was sitting on top of the wall ready to jump. I had got over and was hanging by my fingertip when a rather amused voice stopped us in our tracks. 'Do you always leave the hostel this way?'

Lily replied that it was good exercise, while I slid down, doing my knees no good at all. We brushed ourselves down and walked sedately up the lane.

Being late back was a bind. The warden would keep us waiting in the dark for a few minutes before she opened the door. Then we would have to sign the late book.

Three nights late in a week and we received a right ticking-off. Three nights in succession and we were in real trouble. The Ipswich office would be informed and the girl or girls would report there for a good lecture.

Very occasionally if the lateness persisted the girl would be moved to another hostel, with a warning to mend her ways.

Lingering at the gate with the boyfriend was often

the reason for being late. It had been much nicer when the boys had been allowed to call for us and wait in the recreation room until we were ready.

One evening Sybil had a date with a rather religious young man. A lot of us were gathered around the piano singing the latest songs being played by Molly. Sybil requested that we sang something a bit more sober when her young man called for her, so when he arrived we were demurely singing 'Onward Christian Soldiers'. I think he was most impressed.

Then everything changed. Barbara and Molly were having their supper when they heard a girl screaming outside. They rushed out to find her being attacked. The man ran off and the girl, though shaken, was unharmed. After that rather nasty incident no man was allowed beyond the gate. Hence the rush down the drive every night.

One time Lily got into trouble for being late following an evening she and Barbara spent at the pub. They had one drink and then another, and when they had not returned by 10.30 pm the door was locked.

When they finally turned up, the under-warden Miss Rose let them in. 'You two are very late. Please sign the book and then go to bed as quietly as you can.'

When they were halfway up the stairs Miss Rose called them back. 'You have not signed the book.

Please come back and do so.'

Lily took the pen and slowly wrote *IN* using very large letters that almost filled one page.

Miss Rose was not amused. 'Wait here you two. I shall have to inform the warden of your bad behaviour.'

The two did not wait around. They were out of the door and running up the drive.

From then on it was chaos. After she was informed, the warden woke Billy who in turn woke me and Bobby's friend Peggy to ask whether either of us had any idea where these two might have gone. The answer being 'no', they then woke Jack to help in the search.

Eventually the girls were found in the wood, tired and very tearful. They were given hot cocoa and a bed in Miss Rose's room for the night.

Next morning they spent an hour or two with the warden in her office, being given a good talking-to and promising to mend their ways. As for me, I was just glad to have my friend back. Peace reigned once more at the Old Rectory.

The Land Girls' Rally

JANUARY 1943 was a very sad month for us at the Old Rectory. Our friend Edna Girling was killed at work, attempting to clear a clogged-up straw baler while the machine was still running.

We were all sent to our homes. My dad had heard the news and just opened his arms for me to fall into.

Girls living a long distance from Halesworth went with girls who lived nearer and the Rectory was closed for a day.

It overwhelmed us all, nothing mattered any more, it was a very unhappy time. We did as we were told – got up in the morning, had breakfast, went to work, came home and ate our meal, hungry after working all day. Then we sat around till bedtime.

This went on for a while then one evening our warden came into the dining room. 'Now girls, when you have finished your meal, I want all of you to get ready and go out. It doesn't matter where or how long you go out, but you are all to go. Is that clear?' So we went.

We never forgot our friend, but things slowly got better and soon it was spring. My 21st birthday was April 30th, so someone suggested having a party after lights out in the big bedroom. It was not much bigger than ours except there were eight beds and the added attraction was a fire-escape ladder that was very useful late at night when we wanted to nip to the fish shop for bags of chips.

We gathered together a few goodies for the party. We had bottles of Tizer, biscuits, sweets (I saved my ration), a large tin of American peanuts, bread and cheese (from the kitchen) and a large Swiss roll my Mother had sent me. There were as many bags of chips as Joyce Berry could carry, as she had volunteered to nip down the ladder and run to the fish shop.

It was a very memorable 21st party that we all enjoyed. To finish off, the girls were quietly singing *Happy Birthday to You* when the door opened and Miss Rose came in. 'Will all those girls who do not belong to this room please go to their own.' Without a murmur we went. As I got into bed I thought what a lovely 21st birthday I had had. Nothing was ever said about the party but a few days later the ladder was removed, never to be put back again. No more chips for us after lights out.

The next interesting thing to occur was the Rally held in Ipswich. Here are the details taken from the *Land Girl Magazine* dated August 1943.

Pride and enthusiasm, music and friendliness, these were the key-notes of our Rally held in Ipswich on one of the loveliest days of summer. Some 600 Land Girls, proud of their force and the honour paid them by a visit from Lord and Lady Woolton, and led by a band of Royal Marines marched gaily through Ipswich to the Public Hall to join a large gathering of representatives, employers and friends.

Our chairman Lady Cranworth introduced the Minister of Food, who, though his speech was throughout of a most delightful informality, stressed the vital necessity of maintaining a high standard of efficiency and keenness in our work, as members of the 4th line of defence. We were additionally lucky in having Miss Brew (headquarters) who made a charming and most helpful speech.

Lord Cranworth speaking as a satisfied employer said what he and other farmers needed were more land girls. Mr S. Paul, Chairman of the W.A.E.C. thanked the speakers and a special message was sent by our Chairman to employers who had allowed their land girls time off for the very important occasion and to those girls whose work had prevented them from attending.

Then came the presentation of Good Service Badges by Lord and Lady Woolton. The afternoon ended with a variety entertainment by land girls from many of our hostels. They put on a most excellent show which was thoroughly enjoyed by everyone. There were choruses by girls from Blombyle Hall and Henstead Hostel, solo singing by Miss P Rufford and

Miss V. Stevens, piano solos by Miss May Rose and Miss M. Leeks, a monologue by Miss J. Vokes, an accordion solo by Miss C. Gibson, tap-dancing by Miss M. Turlon and a recitation of one of her own poems by Miss B. Miles.

Mrs Sunderland-Taylor reminded everyone present that Miss J. Woodgate (Asst. Labour Officer, W.A.E.C.) would broadcast on July 25th, an honour of which we were all, and especially 'her hostel girls' very proud.

A raffle for the Benevolent Fund of a second-hand bicycle (painted a lovely shade of land army green), a rabbit, a sun hat (pattern obtainable from Henstead hostel), 100 cigarettes and an orange, brought in £11 8s., and £2.14s. was raised by contributions.

Then on Sunday August 29th a W.L.A. broadcast on the Home Service was to deal with matters of considerable interest to Women's Land Army members, including the uniform rationing arrangements for the new clothing year beginning in September. There were to be W.L.A. correspondence courses in agriculture and horticulture and the introduction of the Women's Land Army Proficiency Tests.

The test gave Lily and me something to think about, but not yet.

Transport

TRAINS and buses were a bind to some of us girls. Getting from Halesworth to Ipswich was often a gamble. Maybe we were just not organized, as most of the time we had a rush to the station to catch the train. By the time we had purchased our ticket and hurried over the bridge to the other platform the train would be in the station.

While the passengers cooled their heels and the guard looked at his watch, the driver would be urging us to hurry up and threatening not to wait for us next time, which he always did. Having got on at Beccles, the girls from Henstead hostel were usually on this train, among them my younger sister Elsie. We would chatter non-stop on the journey home. We were given a few rations to take home of which our Mother was very glad: 2 oz butter, 2 oz sugar and a twist of tea. It was not a lot, but every little helped in wartime.

On the subject of trains, one Saturday afternoon trip to Lowestoft ended at the Beccles police station for Lily and me. It all began pleasantly enough. We had a wander round the shops, popped in for a cup of tea, then went back to the station in good time to catch the last train back to Halesworth.

A train came into the station. To be quite sure it was the right one we asked a lady porter, 'Is this the Halesworth train?'

'No it isn't,' she replied.

We watched the train slowly leaving the platform, when the porter dashed over. 'Was it the train *to* Halesworth you wanted?'

'Yes.'

'I am sorry, that was it,' she said.

We did not have time to reply, but dashed out of the station and jumped into a taxi. 'Follow that train,' we told the startled driver.

'Where to, Miss?'

'Can you catch the train up at Beccles, please?'

'I'll have a go,' and we were off.

We could not believe it, but as we drove into Beccles station, the tail end of the train was disappearing from view.

We paid the driver. We could have been marooned at Lowestoft *with* money, instead here we were at Beccles with very little left. We decided to pay a visit to the police station. The sergeant on duty, although sympathetic, did not really know what to do with us. He jokingly offered us a cell for the night. We declined that offer. 'There is an American convoy passing through here at midnight. I could get you a lift on that as they are going to Halesworth.' We definitely turned that offer down.

'Well Girls, I will have a word with my wife. I am sure she will be pleased to have you stay the night. Won't be long.' A few minutes later he was back. We had a bed.

'Now Girls, are you on a private farm or in a hostel? If it's the latter, I had better have your warden's name and phone number.'

We gave him the details and the conversation went as follows:

'Good evening. Am I speaking to Mrs Hill, Warden, Old Rectory, Halesworth? This is Beccles police station. I have two of your girls here, Lily and Irene.'

Pause.

'No Madam, they missed the last train to Halesworth and came here for help. My wife will give the girls a bed for the night and they can catch the first train back in the morning.'

The sergeant said that she wanted a word with one of us and with that he handed the phone to me.

'How dare you miss the train? I shall expect you first thing in the morning.' The phone was slammed down. Nonetheless we both slept well. After we had eaten a good breakfast we went back to face a very irate warden.

Buses were not much better. A trip to Southwold

resulted in five of us having a long walk home. The attraction at Southwold was a roller-skating rink and a canteen where land girls were made welcome. On this particular day we enjoyed a pleasant hour on the rink, then made our way to the canteen for a welcome cup of tea. To our delight jam tarts were on the menu, a feast indeed. We had plenty of time, the last bus left at 6.30 pm.

Some time later we heard the bus coming and dashed out, to see it disappearing down the road. It took us three hours to walk the nine miles, the thought of our tea keeping us going.

By the time we walked into the Old Rectory it was 9.30 pm. Miss Rose was waiting for us. 'What a pity, I have just cleared your tea away. You really must come in at the appropriate time. It will have to be bread and cheese and cocoa for you girls.'

We had our bread and cheese and cocoa, then went to bed and dreamed of the tea we should have had.

Our Wardens

WARDENS were in charge at W.L.A Hostels. During the course of our stay at the Old Rectory we had three wardens and one under-warden. Our first was Mrs H. I really cannot recall much about her except that she was a rather quiet lady. Maybe dealing with thirty lively girls was too much for her. I do not think she stayed very long. We came home one day to be told Mrs H. had left and we had a new warden in her place.

Getting ready for our evening meal, we were all speculating as to why Mrs H. had left, but more importantly what was the new warden like? We soon found out. In the middle of our meal this stranger walked in. She clapped her hands for silence and the conversation that followed went something like this:

'Good evening Girls. I am your new warden. My name is Miss Lloyd. I don't know why your other warden left, but you won't get rid of me so easily. I have a hand of velvet and a hand of steel. It's up to you which hand I use. If you behave yourselves, then I shall use my hand of velvet and we shall all get along fine. But if you misbehave, I shall not hesitate to use my hand of steel. Is that quite clear? Right! Now I want your names, both names please, not just your surnames. I shall start at that table in the corner.'

Unfortunately this happened to be our table, and Lily was late again. Miss Lloyd took our names and moved to the next table. She had just finished when Lily dashed in. A very angry warden snapped, 'What's your name, girl? You are late.'

Lily muttered, 'Baguley' and sat down. She began to eat her meal.

'You were supposed to tell Miss Lloyd both your names. Hadn't you better go and tell her?'

'No fear, I'm hungry,' and she went on eating.

Later we were getting ready to go out when Joyce Berry came to our room. 'Miss Lloyd wants you to go to her office now, Lily; well, I think it's you she wants. I was told to tell *Beager Ooley* to report to the office.'

When Lily came back she was indignant. She had had two tellings off, one for being late and one for giving the wrong name! After that we were on our best behaviour, not wanting Miss Lloyd to use her hand of steel. It was a very quiet hostel for a time.

In view of that we were very surprised a couple of weeks later to be told that Miss Lloyd had left and we now had another warden. We tried to get Anne to tell us what this one was like but to no avail. 'Wait and see,' we were told.

We did not have long to wait. The new warden

walked into the dining room with a smile on her face. 'Good evening Girls. My name is Mrs Hill and I am quite sure we are all going to get along fine. If you have any worries or would just like a chat, please come and see me, my door will always be open.' She was as good as her word and she would always listen.

The only time we saw Mrs Hill very annoyed was over some loganberries that grew near the bike shed. Some of us had watched them getting riper and more luscious every day, until one morning we could not resist them and ate the lot. That evening we were summoned to be in the recreation room at 7.00 pm. In walked a very angry Mrs Hill. She talked and we listened.

'For some time now I have watched my lovely loganberries getting ripe. This morning I took my dish to pick them. I could not believe it, they had all gone. Now I want the girl or girls to please own up. If they do I will say no more about it, but if no one owns up, I shall keep you here until you do.' Silence reigned.

The time ticked on. It was 7.15 then 7.30, everyone was getting restless. I felt very guilty, but the others did not say anything, so I kept quiet. By now Mrs Hill was looking very angry indeed. Another few minutes went by and then she got to her feet. 'I am very disappointed with you all. Now get out of my sight.' We fled!

None of the other girls had said a word, and I am sure they knew who we were. We did own up eventually, but by then Mrs Hill had forgotten the incident and she took it all in good part.

Now a word about our under-warden, Miss Rose. She was a very nice lady, quiet and dignified. Before the war she had travelled a great deal and had been to many places abroad. However, she never talked about the places she had visited. When she was asked about anywhere, her answer was always the same, 'Well, I never really noticed.' What a shame to have seen so much and noticed nothing. But everyone liked Miss Rose, she was a friend to us all.

Potatoes, Sugar Beet and Muck Spreading

AS THE NEWSPAPERS kept reporting, it was vital to grow as much food as we could in wartime. Potatoes and sugar-beet were both essential commodities. Sugar was needed and potatoes would always fill a gap to eke out our rations.

As far as I was concerned, picking potatoes was a boring, back-aching job. We also planted the seed potatoes and opened potato clamps. The clamps were huge mounds of potatoes covered in straw, then earth. These were then left usually until well into the winter. Our first day on the clamps was quite an eye-opener.

When we arrived on the farm six of us were given three pick-axes and three forks. It soon became clear why we needed the pick-axes. The clamp was hard as concrete. Most of the time the potatoes were perfect in the clamps but we did open one clamp to find that the majority of the potatoes had rotted. We were told we must sort them over to see if any were worth saving. The smell was awful, and after fifteen minutes work we had to have five minutes break. When we eventually finished sorting the clamp we did not have many potatoes worth saving.

On one clamp we found dozens of little new potatoes. We put them aside and shared them out at the end of the day. My mother was delighted to get new potatoes at that time of year.

Pulling and topping sugar-beet in freezing cold weather was tough on our hands – we never wore gloves. I will say this, our hands got used to the cold surroundings and warmed up after a time.

Working outside in winter took some getting used to. Lunch breaks sitting on frozen logs were not much fun. The majority of farmers treated us well. Often we got an invitation to go into the house for a welcome cup of tea.

There was the rare time when we were not welcome. One isolated case springs to mind. It was a freezing cold day. We were sitting on frozen logs to have our lunch wishing, I might add, that we were anywhere but here when Barbara dropped her flask and broke it. I went to the house hoping to get her a cup of tea. I knocked on the door and explained what had happened. I was told to wait. A few minutes later a mug was thrust in my hand. I was a bit taken aback to be told, 'pump's round the corner,' and the door was shut in my face. As it turned out, the pump was frozen, so we did not even get a drink of water. We shared the remaining flask so we had a drink each.

One day we went on strike. Our job for the day

was pulling and topping sugar-beet. It really was an awful day. It was snowing hard with a cold wind blowing. When we arrived at the field, we took one look and refused to get out of the bus. The snow was deep, the sugar-beet could not be seen, we were on strike.

Billy did not believe us. Her reply of, 'Nonsense, Girls,' did not help at all.

Billy got off the bus, marched briskly onto the field and got down to some hard work. We sat watching her for about ten minutes, then as one got off the bus and joined in. That was our first and our last strike.

Another chore was muck-spreading for which Billy advised us to 'wear rubber boots or your lace-up boots. Do not wear shoes.'

Alighting from the bus, the reason for her request became clear. Heaps of muck were dotted over the field everywhere. We were handed a fork with instructions to work in pairs.

'Spread the muck evenly and do remember to clean your fork when you have finished for the day.'

Lily and I looked at each other then at the heaps of muck with distaste. Seeing our expressions Billy had a quick comment to make: 'Now come along Gals, don't look upon this as a chore but a healthy exercise.' As far as she was concerned that was what it was. As for us, we had our own title for the job: we were pilots. After all, that's what we did, 'pilot' here and 'pilot' there. The worst job of all was unloading the trailers and shoving the muck out onto the field. We really were up to our knees in muck.

When we went to a farm next to a battle training area the army were there on manoeuvres, and we were looking forward to having a laugh with the boys. Billy, however, was quick to point out the disadvantages of having soldiers all over the place.

'Before you get too excited, think carefully. There will be occasions when you will need to go off the field. With the army everywhere you will have to be careful. I suggest three or four of you keep together. The soldiers will most likely be in camouflage behind bushes, trees or in ditches.'

Billy was right. They seemed to be everywhere. During the morning some dressed as the enemy ran across our field, followed a short time later by the army. They all disappeared into the wood. Nella protested to Billy, that in no way did she want anyone with her and dashed off on her own. On her return we were told of a perfect place she had found. A circle of bushes over there to the right. However when we looked, her circle of bushes had moved! Nella could not believe it.

At midday a gang of us went off together, determined that we would find a safe place. We found a deep ditch with bushes along the top of one side. Perfect, we thought and slid down into it. Pulling up our dungarees we got a shock when what we thought were bushes were in reality soldiers in tin hats with camouflage. Six heads appeared. A very pleasant voice inquired, 'Can we help you out girls?'

With as much dignity as we could muster under the circumstances, we declined their offer and climbed out, determined to be more careful in future.

During our tea break we were invited to have a ride in their tank. Lily accepted, taking her flask top of tea with her. We watched her get into the tank. The top was closed and they moved off.

The tank went over a bump, came to an abrupt stop, the top opened and out came Lily followed by a soldier, both covered in tea, while Lily was now holding an empty cup. I must say the soldier was looking none too happy.

We think the boys got the message; they never spied on us again. After a week of muck spreading we all agreed it was not one of our favourite jobs.

Hedging and Ditching

UNDER this heading we did a variety of jobs. We cut and laid hedges, cleaned ditches, cleared waste land, cut down trees, cleaned round smelly ponds and laid drainage pipes. Cutting a hedge was quite straight-forward, laying a hedge was much more difficult. A good stout branch had to be cut three parts through and then entwined to make a solid hedge. There were a few mistakes when we first tackled this job and many a good branch fell to the ground. But we learned quickly and were soon making hedges which lasted many years.

Ditches were a challenge, filled with dock leaves, paper, nettles and blackberry bushes. Some were full of stagnant water.

We cleared a lot of waste land and cut down trees. For this job we had to learn another skill, how to use a cross-cut saw. This was extremely hard work. Laying drainage pipes was another job we had to get used to. Not a job for the faint hearted.

One time when a gang of us were hedging we had finished on the first field and were gathering our things to walk up the lane to the next field. Although the fields were adjacent, a rather wide water-filled ditch divided them. Jumping it was not an option we considered. Billy in her wisdom thought otherwise.

'Now girls I'm quite sure we can all clear this ditch, it will save a lot of walking.'

I was appalled. I was five-foot nothing with short legs. I would never do it. My nerves took over. I had visions of broken limbs or at least lying prone in the ditch.

Billy stayed to see us across, and the others all cleared the ditch with ease. Just two of us were left, me and Rene Seaward who incidently looked as nervous as me. Both of us hesitated until Billy got impatient. 'Hurry up you two, we haven't got all day.' That spurred me on. I went back a bit, took a flying leap, cleared the ditch with ease. As for Rene, I am afraid she fell in!

Another hedging job almost turned into a disaster. We were told by the farmer to burn all the rubbish and we had a huge fire going. Jesse was coming up to the fire with a forkful of rubbish, when Billy dashed over and took it from her. She shouted to us to stop work while she took the fork to the far end of the field. She then told us to go two fields away and wait. She had seen some sort of device amongst the rubbish and was going to telephone the police.

After Billy had gone we stood around discussing how many of the bomb squad would arrive. We could not believe it when one policeman rode up on his bike in a leisurely fashion. 'Hello, what's all this about some device you have found?'

Billy took him across the field and pointed it out. The man took one look, got on his bike, shouted to Billy, 'Keep them gals well away,' and pedalled like mad down the lane. We did not have the satisfaction of seeing the bomb squad as Billy decided to take us home early.

One good thing came from it, we got a bath before the others came back.

On a different occasion we were working at Blythburgh when an enemy bomber crashed on the common. Our first instinct was to go and see if we could be of any help. Billy stopped us in our tracks. 'Stay where you are. No one is to move. Is that clear?'

Seconds later there was a deafening noise when the plane blew up, with bits and pieces falling very close to us. It was rumoured that people who had gone to help were injured, which was very sad. We were grateful that Billy had given us those orders and that we had obeyed them.

We had a lovely surprise one morning, having just arrived at work ready to start cleaning ditches. A convoy of American lorries came along and slowed down. A cheerful voice from the first lorry called out, 'Here you are, Honey,' and six oranges came over the hedge and went into the ditch. The other lorries followed suit and soon we had quite a lot of fruit. We all worked hard and cleared that ditch in record time. It was a relief to find it dry, and soon our precious fruit was on the bank.

Soon after, Billy came along to see how we were getting on. She was quite taken aback at the speed we had worked. She looked at her watch and then at us. 'I don't know what brought this rash of work on, but I shall expect this speed every day,' she said.

We thought it best to own up and tell her about the oranges. She seemed very annoyed at first, but then gave a grin and we knew it was all right. We shared our precious oranges, Billy included. They were delicious; we had not seen as many oranges in such a long, long time.

Threshing

THIS was not a job for the faint-hearted; it was dirty, dusty and very noisy. There were also rats and mice to contend with. Our first day was a bit of an ordeal, but like everything else we had to get used to it.

I was put on the chaff and Lily was sweeping up the cavings. We saw that the men had bits of string tied round their trouser-legs, just above the ankles. I ventured to ask the reason for this. Their reply of, 'You'll soon find out, Missie,' didn't satisfy me at all.

Everything became clear when a mouse ran up Lily's trouser leg. She was terrified and began to dance about trying to shake the little creature down. To her relief, one of the men jumped from the stack and slapped her sharply on the leg, killing the mouse which fell out from her trouser bottom.

The men thought it a huge joke. 'Does that answer your question about the string, Missie?' It certainly did, and string became our priority. We were never without it.

The chaff bags were very heavy. I had to fling the bag over my shoulder and stagger with it to the barn. My back and arms soon ached with the strain. The nearer the barn the better it was for me, otherwise by the time I returned, the next bag was almost full. It was a never-ending job. Rats and mice were a menace as the corn stack got lower. The rodents began to jump out sometimes landing on my shoulder, other times scuttling round my feet. I was terrified of them. The men were only too glad to kill them, as they got 2*d*. a tail.

It was a relief when Lily and I were taken off those jobs and put to work on the straw stack which by this time was quite high. My job was in the bully hole and Lily was higher up. The straw came up the conveyor belt to where I was standing. I then forked up the straw, passed it to Lily who in turn passed it to Old George who was putting the roof on.

Two stacks were often built side by side with very little space in between and on one very windy day Old George was blown off the stack and unfortunately fell between the two. It was panic stations until he was hauled out.

As the roof began to take shape there was no room for Lily and Old George, so I had to get down and Lily took my place in the bully hole. Everything had to stop, the conveyor belt was taken away and a ladder put there for me to use. I had to turn round and go down backwards, with plenty of encouragement from the men. 'Steady now Gal, you're nearly there, down you come,' There were willing hands if I wobbled a bit.

We went with the threshing tackle from farm to farm, one of which was kept by two sisters at Wenhaston. One worked on the farm, the other kept house. We were always invited in at midday for a cup of tea and very glad we were to have it, until one day we were sitting waiting for our tea when their cat jumped up on to the table and drank from the milk jug. The woman did not seem to notice, and just went on pouring the tea.

'Excuse me, your cat is drinking from the milk jug.'

'It don't matter, she always do that.'

It might not have mattered to her, but it put me off my tea. As we had another three weeks' work at this farm and many more cups of tea to drink, Lily and I looked at each other and then drank up. After all, threshing was thirsty work.

We arrived one morning to be told we were in charge of the straw stack. The men were working elsewhere. Feeling a bit nervous, we first sorted out the corners, then got stuck in. As time went on, we became confident we were doing a good job. Some time later the sisters came to inspect progress. They walked round the stack, then both grinned. 'This is not a bad effort girls, but we must say it's the funniest shaped stack we have ever seen.' When we came down we could see what they meant. But for a couple of 'town gals' it really was not such a bad effort.

At Wissett we worked for six weeks at Mr N's

farm. As soon as we arrived he took us to see his dog. It scared me, it was the biggest St Bernard I had ever seen. 'His name is Rover,' we were told. Mr N. thought the world of his dog. A dozen times a day he would come and ask us where Rover was. Our reply of, 'He's in his kennel, Mr N.' seemed to make him happy.

He was rather an eccentric man but very kind to us girls. He gave us 2*s*. 6*d*. every Friday and every day a tray of tea was put in the barn with a wooden form for us to sit on. He also had a house-keeper who took Rover for a run each day – or more to the point, Rover took her. The poor woman could be seen most days running to keep up with the dog. I think we were all a bit sorry when our work on his farm was finished and we had to move on.

Some farmers built their stacks in Dutch barns. They were awful to work in, very hot and stuffy. I disliked them very much, but it did save the farmer from having to thatch the stack.

The worst job we ever had was threshing clover. That really was very dirty, the dust getting down our throats and making us cough a lot.

The Proficiency Test

IT WAS 1944 and I had by now been a land girl for one year and seven months. I had worked out in all weathers: the pleasant spring, the hot summer, the delightful autumn and the cold winter.

I loved the variety of work and also the large area we covered. From Halesworth we travelled to Wrentham, Henstead, Wangford, Darsham, Brampton, Wissett, Linstead, Holton, Sutherton, Fressingfield, South Cove, Yoxford, Wenhaston and Blythburgh. A little incident at Blythburgh comes to mind. One lunch break we had a look round the church and found this note on the door:

Please close the door, as birds fly in and die of thirst. When we came out we did make sure the door was firmly closed.

This year was eventful for three main reasons. The first being the D–Day Landings, the second was when the bomb dump at Metfield blew up and the third was the Proficiency Test. As far as the D–Day Landings were concerned, no more need be said as everyone followed the war very closely.

Now the bomb dump at Metfield. The date was July 15th, the time 7.30 pm. It was one of the biggest explosions to occur in Suffolk during the Second World War. About 1,250 tons of high-explosive bombs were detonated, destroying five bombers and killing five airmen.

Most of us girls were sitting on our beds or getting ready to go out when the explosion happened. It was very frightening. It shook the Rectory and we got showered with plaster from the ceiling. When we found out later what had occurred we were just glad to have been a few miles away from it.

When we were told about the proficiency tests, Lily, Jesse Mills and I thought about it and decided against it. Billy took the decision out of our hands by putting our names down.

'I am not ready,' I told Billy.

'If you're not ready now, Gibbs, you never will be. It's too late, your names have been handed in.'

My attitude after that was, oh well! I shall either pass or fail. With that logic I stopped worrying and began to look forward to the challenge. The tests were held on three Wednesdays in October. Lily, Jesse and I were entered for the 25th.

The day was dry and fine. I had felt very nervous beforehand but once I got going I was fine. First, we had to pull and top two rows of sugar beet, then we had to spread two rows of muck, making sure we cleaned our forks afterwards. We had to identify plants and weeds, and answer a great many farming questions. We were given tea in the large barn while we were being assessed and marked. It was with great relief the three of us heard we had passed.

When the *East Suffolk News Sheet* for November 1944 was printed it was mainly about the proficiency test. This is what the newsletter said:

In the midst of a spell of very wet weather we were lucky enough to have three comparatively fine Wednesdays. On October 11th the tests were held at Columbyne Hall, on the 18th at Sutton Hoo and 25th at Kelsale Lodge.

After the initial stage fright had worn off, the entrants seemed to enjoy themselves.

The high standard of the results certainly showed that the land girls must have taken an intelligent interest in their work.

The newsheet also included the results of the East Suffolk hostel land girls' labour during the year, a record of which 'they may be justly proud'.

During the winter months sixty miles of hedging was done by the girls. This included some drainage schemes.
Stacks thatched for W.A.E.C. with mats 37
Stacks thatched for private farms   35
                              Total 72 stacks.
Thatch mats made for W.A.E.C.   12,793 yards
Thatch mats made for private farmers 12,823 yards
        Total 25,616 yards, just over 14 miles.

Hoeing approx. 1,000 acres sugar beet have been chopped and thinned.
Other hoeing over 670 acres.

WOMEN'S LAND ARMY PROFICIENCY CERTIFICATE.

THIS IS TO CERTIFY THAT

Miss Irene Gibbs.   W.L.A. No. 77475.

HAS BEEN AWARDED A PROFICIENCY BADGE

IN   Field Work.

Date October 1944.   Signed   G. Denman.
on behalf of the Women's Land Army.

Goodbye to the Old Rectory

1945 STARTED much the same as any other. January was cold, wet, with some very bleak mornings. Nothing much had changed, black-out curtains and rationing were still very much in force. Oranges were few and bananas were a thing of the past. I made up my mind that when bananas were once again in the shops, I was going to sit down and eat one very slowly and really enjoy it.

Lily and I were still at the Rectory and planned to stay there until we left the W.L.A. But things have a habit of changing and the morning of May 8th 1945 changed everything. We were having our breakfast when our warden came into the dining room. 'Girls, girls, wonderful news. The War is over!'

As one, Lily, Kay, Iris and I rushed out of the room, out of the Rectory and on to the Market Place. We were calling to anyone who cared to listen, at that early hour, that the war was over.

On reaching the Market Place we stood outside the King's Arms Hotel and sang 'Ave Maria'. It was very moving, a moment to cherish, 7.15 am on V.E. (Victory in Europe) Day.

A bedroom window at the hotel was opened and

the angry voice of Mr Gooch the landlord cut our song short. 'What the devil is all that noise about?'

Rather meekly we told him the news. 'In that case stay where you are and I will come down and let you in. I must buy you girls a drink.'

It was gin and tonics all round then back to finish our breakfast. We expected a ticking off but our warden was much too happy for that. It was the rest of the day off for us, back to work and reality next day.

It was another three months before V.J. (Victory over Japan) Day. Now we could all begin to relax a little and look to the future.

Now there were Italian prisoners of war billeted a few miles from Halesworth. Most of them were put to work on the land. Although we girls were not allowed to work with them, we did see them working on nearby farms.

Things were moving very fast and one day the blow fell. Our lovely Rectory was going to be sold. We would all have to find other hostels to go to.

A list was put on the board of hostels with vacancies. There was nothing that appealed to Lily and me until we saw that a hostel at Little Hothfield in Kent had four places. Lily and I decided to accept and asked Kay and Iris if they would consider coming with us. They both agreed and as none of us had ever been to Kent it was a challenge.

As well as leaving our friends behind, we were going to be sorry to leave the people of Halesworth who had been very kind to thirty young land girls for more than three years. They had put up with the bell which was rung every night and could be heard for miles around, and they had put up with us girls tearing back to the Rectory at night hoping to get in before the door was locked.

Our feeling for Halesworth was shown in the song we had made up.

We shall always remember
When this war comes to an end
We'll be coming back to Halesworth
Where these happy days we spend.
We'll work as hard as can be
Till that day of victory,
Then we'll all come back to Halesworth
When the war ends.

We shall always remember
It was on a Saturday morn
We were on our way to Darsham
Where we should have threshed some corn.
But at Bramfield we got stuck
With no petrol – oh! what luck,
We'll all come back to Halesworth
When the war ends.

We cut those hedges too
Though the cattle beet were few
Even though we grumble
It's the life for me and you.
We'll work as hard as can be
Till that day of victory,
Then we'll all come back to Halesworth
When the war ends.

Now our little song is ending
And we just want you to know
It's the story of some land girls
Who worked for Winston, Frank and Joe.
We'll work as hard as can be
Till that day of victory,
Then we'll all come back to Halesworth
When the war ends.

A few nights before we left Halesworth, we were all invited to the Picture House by the residents. When the film was over a message came on the screen. It was to the land girls from the people of Halesworth, thanking us for the hard work we had done and wishing us luck in the future. I don't think there was a dry eye amongst us as we made our way back to the Rectory.

I had also been lucky in working for the Pearsons from April to September 1945. Their farm was a short

75

walk from the Rectory and it had been a pleasure working for them.

Anyway, we now had to say goodbye, and we were quite looking forward to something new. It was, 'Kent, here we come.'

Kent

WE WERE sent travel warrants and instructions about times and trains to catch: first to London, Liverpool St, across to Waterloo, then on to Ashford, Kent. The four of us were quite looking forward to the journey.

When we arrived at Ashford we boarded a bus to Hothfield. We asked the driver to put us off near to the W.L.A. hostel.

It was a surprise when the bus stopped at the entrance to a wood. 'Here you are girls, through the wood and you'll come to your hostel.' With a cheery 'good luck' the bus pulled away. For a second the four of us stood still taking in the surroundings – nothing but trees. At that moment I felt quite homesick for the Old Rectory.

Without a word we started off through the wood. We soon came to a pub, 'The Thanet Inn'. 'It is somewhere to come for a shandy,' I ventured. No answer from the other three. We strode on in silence. A bit later we came to an army camp. There were plenty of offers to help us with our luggage. However, we declined their help and went on our way.

In a clearing we came to the hostel and went in. We met the warden whose name remained unknown, and also a Mrs Mac, the cook. It soon became obvious we would not be together; all of us were in separate rooms. I soon unpacked and went to find the others. After our meal we took a stroll to the pub for a refreshing shandy. As we walked in a voice behind the bar called out, 'No beer!'

'What, no beer?' shouted Lil.

'*No beer*,' repeated the very irate voice behind the bar.

We fled. There was nothing else to do but go back, have supper and turn in.

Next thing I knew I was woken, told to dress and go to the kitchen for breakfast. The other girls in the room were still sleeping. I looked at my watch, it was 5.15 am. What was going on?

I marched downstairs, followed by the other three, plus the land girl we had met the previous day.

We were told, 'As you are rookies, your job this week is the tomato harvest and that means a 6.30 am start.

Lily spoke out sharply. 'We are not rookies, we have three and a quarter years' service behind us and, more to the point, have just finished the corn harvest in Suffolk, which entailed not only very hard work but also long hours. We do not think it right that we are the only ones getting up at this hour while the rest of the girls are still sleeping.'

'In that case I shall have to inform the warden.'

The girl marched angrily out of the kitchen. The warden's verdict was, 'If you refuse to go to work, I suggest you report your grievances to the secretary at Canterbury.'

A quick discussion and we all agreed on that option. At Canterbury the secretary was waiting, the warden having telephoned her.

'I understand you girls have refused to go to work. I will not tolerate that kind of behaviour. If you don't like it in Kent, I suggest you go back to Suffolk. I will not give you travel warrants, you will have to pay your own fares.' We were dismissed with no chance to explain.

I proposed we spent that day in Canterbury and went back to Suffolk the following day. We had a splendid time, making sure we arrived back at the hostel in time for our evening meal. However, things did not work in our favour. The warden was waiting for us. 'Where have you girls been? The secretary had a change of heart, she came over this afternoon with your travel warrants. She was most annoyed to find you had not returned.' She had waited for a time then left.

It was a relief to get the warrants. We thanked the warden and told her we would leave first thing next day. 'I don't think so. You are to go at once.'

We packed and left. Once more through the wood. This time the question uppermost in our minds was where were we going to sleep? Ipswich seemed a long way away. We boarded the first bus that came along, destination Maidstone.

On our arrival we went to the railway station hoping to get a train to London. No more trains to London until the morning, we were told. We went to the waiting room to discuss our next move. The remains of a fire still glowed in the grate and the room was warm and cosy. 'We'll be fine here,' Lily decided. We agreed and settled down for the night.

We were soon awakened from our complacency, when the station master walked in. 'Sorry girls, you can't stay here.' However much we pleaded the man was adamant.

'It's more than my job's worth,' we were told. 'But I won't have you girls walking the streets. Try and find somewhere to stay. If not, come back here at 9.00 pm and I will see what I can do.'

We thanked him and left. We had no luck and returned at the agreed time. We were taken to a siding. The station master unlocked three carriages. 'You can stay here. I shall have to lock you in, but will let you out in time to get an early train in the morning.'

With a quiet 'good night' he left. It was very cold, and we spent most of the night moving about trying to get warm. It was a relief to catch the early train and we were soon on our way to London.

There we had breakfast at a Lyons Corner House, then a train to Ipswich and home. Waiting for each of us was a letter from Mrs Sunderland Taylor, 'See me in my office Thursday morning.' We were not looking forward to that.

Hope House, Ipswich

ALTHOUGH we were very glad to be back in Ipswich, Kay, Iris, Lily and I regretted that we had had such a short stay in Kent. We did feel, however, that the secretary should have given us a chance to put our point across.

When we went to see Mrs Sunderland Taylor, Lily was determined to state exactly what had happened and I was very glad to let her do the talking because she was better at it than me.

Mrs Sunderland Taylor heard her out, then it was her turn. 'Why did you not think to ring this office? Something could have been worked out. I do not like my girls having to spend the night in a railway carriage. Well now, Gibbs and Baguley, I will give you two a choice: you can either live at home and work in the Ipswich gang, or you can go to Hope House in Ipswich.'

A quick discussion and we opted for Hope House. 'You will report to the warden at 6.30 pm on Sunday.' That gave us a long weekend before we started work again.

When we arrived at Hope House and knocked on the warden's door, a familiar voice bade us enter. Mrs

Hill, our warden from the Old Rectory, was now warden at Hope House. She was as pleased to see us as we were to see her.

Hope House was a much larger place than the Rectory. Hope House Orphanage, also known as East Suffolk Girls Home had originally been founded by Miss Harriet Isham-Grimwade in 1875 at Church Street, St Clement's.

In 1883 the orphanage moved into new buildings at 158 Foxhall Road. Girls in the house were trained for domestic service and to do all the work of the house. A matron was in charge of them. The orphanage was closed in 1940 and was sold in 1942. After that it became a Women's Land Army hostel.

One room in the house that intrigued me was the 'quiet room' in which the activity was far from quiet. It was in here we did our ironing, talked, listened to music, wrote letters or just sat about and relaxed. There was a nice atmosphere about it.

One Sunday morning two nuns paid us a visit. Lily and I answered the door. We asked the nuns if we could help them.

'Tell me, do you have a quiet room?' they asked.

'Yes we do.'

'And what do you do in your quiet room?'

My reply of, 'We do our ironing, write letters, listen to music,' seemed to startle the nuns. They first looked surprised, then shocked.

It was then I realized that to them it was still an orphanage. I hastened to explain that it was now a Women's Land Army hostel. A look of relief came over their faces. We took them to the warden's office and she gave them tea. Refreshed, they went on their way.

By October we both decided to put in for our release, with a leaving date of January 12th 1946. As the day approached we had mixed feelings. On the one hand it would be great not having to get up at 6.00 am every weekday morning, on the other hand we would miss the outdoor life. We had learnt a great deal about work on the land, not least that it was very hard work.

Under the heading of field work we had carried out an enormous range of jobs: hoeing, haymaking, harvest, sugar-beet pulling and topping, muck spreading, hedging and ditching, kale and cabbage cutting, stone picking, clearing waste land, cutting down trees, clearing round smelly ponds, drag raking, potato picking, opening potato clamps, fruit picking, building a straw stack, pulling cattle beet, helping to thatch, laying drainage pipes and lime washing a cowshed.

When we left the W.L.A. we received a letter from Queen Elizabeth, now the Queen Mother:

By this personal message, I wish to express to you, Irene Olive Gibbs, my appreciation of your loyal and devoted service as a member of the Women's Land Army, from 8th June 1942 to 12th January 1946.

Your unsparing efforts at a time when the victory of our cause depended on the utmost use of the resources of our land have earned you the country's gratitude.

Elizabeth R.

While I was very proud to have received this letter I was somewhat disappointed not to have been given a gratuity. We left the W.L.A with just the money we had earned for our last week's work. No more.

We had all worn uniforms and had been disciplined like the armed forces. We had lived away from home and undertaken very hard work that had been vital to the nation. Without our work what would Britain have done?

In spite of this disappointment I have never regretted my years in the Land Army.

After 'demob' Lily and I went to work at Grimwade & Ridleys, food and drug packers in Ipswich. However, working indoors was frustrating after our outdoor life and as the weather warmed up we took many an afternoon off to go for a cycle ride in the country.

Before long, of course, we were summoned to the office for a severe reprimand. That was the end of our cycle trips but not of our friendship which, begun in wartime at the Old Rectory, has lasted to the present day.

WOMEN'S LAND ARMY (ENGLAND AND WALES).

RELEASE CERTIFICATE.

The Women's Land Army for England and Wales acknowledges with appreciation the services given by

Miss Irene Gibbs

who has been an enrolled member for the period from

June 8 19*42* to *January 12* 19*46*

and has this day been granted a willing release.

Date *January 13. 1946*

COUNTY SECRETARY, WOMEN'S LAND ARMY.

Postscript:
The Old Rectory 54 Years On

I HAD VISITED Halesworth many times over the years, always intending to call at the Rectory, but had never done so. The opportunity came when Lily's daughter Juanita, with her friend Julie, came over from Maryland, USA for a three-week holiday. A list of places they wished to visit included the Old Rectory. Juanita was keen to see where her mother and I had lived during our Land Army days.

The day we picked for the visit was July 13th. I met them at Ipswich railway station at 10.30 am. The next train to Halesworth would be leaving at 10.50 am, from platform 1, so we did not have much time. I must mention the wheelchair. Lily had been unwell for several weeks; she now felt better but could not walk very far, hence the wheelchair. While Julie queued for tickets (£8 day return), we managed to get the chair folded and onto the train.

We stopped at every station, just like old times. There were changes at Halesworth Station. The bridge we had dashed across so many times had gone, although a new one was to be built in the near future, we were informed. We left the station at a brisk walk, the Rectory being our first stop. Arriving there I went to open the gate but the sound of barking dogs stopped me in my tracks. We calculated there were at least three of them. After a quick discussion we agreed not to venture down the drive. Feeling a bit disappointed we went down Rectory Lane.

The wall surrounding the house seemed higher than I remembered. Did I really climb over that? A little further on we stopped. Lily was certain we could see the house from here, providing we had something to stand on. What better than the wheelchair! We pushed it firmly against the wall, then helped Lily onto the chair. She then had a perfect view. My turn next. I thought the house looked lovely. Juanita was ready with her camera. As she climbed on the chair the sound of a lawn-mower could be heard heading our way. The next minute we heard Juanita's voice: 'Hello there, are you the gardener?'

'No. I live here. May I ask what you are doing?'

She hurriedly explained the reason for her presence. We were delighted to have an invitation to look round the grounds by the owner.

'Please get off whatever you are standing on before you fall. I will meet you in the drive.' When we queried about the dogs, we were assured they would be put in the house.

The front of the house had had a face-lift and the door was a pale yellow rather than brown. The old bell was still there and we were invited to give it a good tug. It really did sound loud. We walked past the lake where we had tried to float an old door which had of course sunk. Was it still at the bottom of the lake? The back of the house looked much the same. Lily pointed to the bedroom window we had climbed out of late one night to see some friends off at the station. It looked a fair way from the ground, although we had had a water butt to land on.

We were pleased to be offered the chance to look round the house.

In the kitchen was a wooden table similar to the one where we had eaten. I could almost see our suppers: a large loaf, a hunk of cheese and a very small piece of butter, and at the other end would be George the cat, sitting on or underneath the table. The gravestones were still there in the pantry. We saw the room used as an office for the warden. The recreation room where we had spent many happy hours reading, writing letters, maybe having a good gossip or listening to Molly or Miss Rose playing tunes on the piano.

Entering the dining room I thought of our cook Anne Frost and the wonderful evening meals we had enjoyed. Lily and I were happy to be given the chance to see our old bedroom. It was hard to believe that six of us had slept in this room. Then a quick look into the other rooms. I was interested to see the one we referred to as the big bedroom (eight beds), in which I had had my late-night feast for my 21st birthday. What fun we had had.

Outside again we took a few more photographs. We were so grateful that the owner let us reminisce for a short while. We walked slowly back up the drive, making sure we closed the gate firmly behind us.

Appendix

Girls who Passed the Proficiency Test

The tests were held on October 11, 18 and 25 1944 at Columbyne Hall, Sutton Hoo and Kelsale respectively. Here are the names of all the girls who passed their proficiency test along with the hostels where they were based.

OCTOBER 11, COLUMBYNE HALL

Columbyne Hall
P. Beck

Wickham Market
G. Coleman, L. Risby, F. Shaw

Freston
M. Bridgeman, V. Brown, E. Hennersay

Helmingham
F. Fordsike, Mrs B. Mayhew

Hope House
K. Haigh, K. McDermont, M. Pearson

Sutton Rectory
I. Harding, C. Swainston

Sutton Hoo
E. Jackson

Hasketon
B. Hardwick, U. Rose, I. Watford

Shelley
I. Milling, M. Old, M. Seammers

Private Farm Old Newton
J. Fisher

OCTOBER 18, BLOMBYLE HALL

Blombyle Hall
S. Baker, F. Barker, M. Battly, B. Buxton, E. Durrant,
E. Elson, E. Fieldhouse, G. Hayes, V. Hill, S. Johnston,
M. Judd, E. Mann, J. Pratt, E. Somers, (DIST) Mrs B. Warner

Campsea Ashe
H. Broadbent, A. Clarke, D. Clarke, H. Fuhy, E. Francis,
M. Grandsome, A. Hudson, G. Rutter, E. Wilks

OCTOBER 25, KELSALE

Halesworth
L. Baguley, I. Gibbs, J. Mills, E. Bailey (DIST)

Herringfleet

Peasenhall
V. Baldry, M. Bloom, K. Boyle, L. Keeble, Mrs M. Long,
M. Prail, J. Whittaker

Henstead
F. Becket, J. Harrold, E. Hutton, E. Snashell

Sutton Hoo
D. Gaylich

Wickham Market
J. Joyce

Leiston
H. Revel

Mettingham
F. Stone

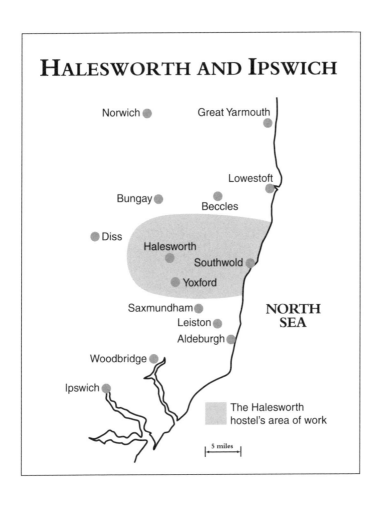

HALESWORTH AND IPSWICH

Norwich

Great Yarmouth

Lowestoft

Bungay

Beccles

Diss

Halesworth

Southwold

Yoxford

Saxmundham

Leiston

Aldeburgh

NORTH SEA

Woodbridge

Ipswich

The Halesworth hostel's area of work

5 miles

Other Books from Old Pond Publishing

A Land Girl's War   JOAN SNELLING
Joan Snelling became a tractor driver during her wartime service in Norfolk. Her book recalls the dangers and tragedies of the period as well as its lighter side and her romance with an RAF pilot. Paperback

Land Girls Gang Up   PAT PETERS
The group of land girls to which Pat Peters belonged in Cornwall were a gang of Londoners who were determined not to be downtrodden by the local farmers. Camaraderie, laughs and friendships to last a lifetime. Paperback

Charismatic Cows & Beefcake Bulls   SONIA KURTA
Sonia Kurta's memories of farm work as a young girl are mostly set in Cornwall on the great Caerhays estate. She joined the Land Army in 1943 and stayed until it was disbanded in 1950. Paperback

In a Long Day   DAVID KINDRED AND ROGER SMITH
Two hundred captioned photographs of farm work and village life in Suffolk 1925-33. Paperback.

We Waved to the Baker   ANDREW ARBUCKLE
A series of childhood memories of escapades on Scottish farm. Nostalgic, amusing and full of warmth. Hardback

Footsteps to the Furrow   ANDREW ARBUCKLE
A portrait of farming life in Fife over the past 100 years showing what it was like for those who worked in the industry. Paperback

A Good Living   HUGH BARRETT
Managing farms from 1938 to 1949, Hugh Barrett encountered a range of characters from war profiteers to ex-miners on Land settlement smallholdings. Paperback

Free complete catalogue:

Old Pond Publishing Ltd
Dencora Business Centre
36 White House Road, Ipswich IP1 5LT, United Kingdom
Phone: 01473 238200
Website: www.oldpond.com